The Journey Begins

The Journey Begins

Vern Rutsala

The University of Georgia Press, Athens

Acknowledgments

The author and the publisher are grateful to the editors of the following periodicals for permission to reprint poems which first appeared in their pages: *Ambit* (London); *American Poetry Review* for "The Journey Begins"; *Chicago Review;* *Esquire* for "The Nursing Home"; *Iowa Review; kayak; Mad River Review; Minnesota Review; New Republic* for "Other Lives"; *New Statesman; New Yorker* for "By the Willamette"; *Northwest Review; Paris Review* for "You"; *Poetry* for "In the Middle," "Unlocking the Door," "January Thaw" (originally "Boxing Day"), "Drinking Late," "Mesh," "Paths," "Quest," and "Like the Poets of Ancient China"; *Poetry Northwest; Poetry NOW* for "Sickness in Childhood"; *Southern Review* for "Quiet Streets" and "Rooms"; *Times Literary Supplement; Tribune* (London).

Library of Congress Catalog Card Number: 76-12681
ISBN: 0-8203-0406-9

The University of Georgia Press, Athens 30602

To Joan

Contents

Investigations

Some days we begin after midnight.
Silence wants voices, rooms long for guests,
we look for the slow conversation
of friends found on the street
like ten-dollar bills. And all the while
birds ride dust in silos; grain elevators
strain to lift their big feet;
we look in books for hands and faces.
Mornings, we stare at dead leaves,
tangle of frozen twigs,
cloud traces, stories written in ice.
We swallow offices and rooms.
Jobs happen to us like accidents.
This goes on no matter how deep our smiles,
no matter how heavy and healthy
the briefcases we carry like pets.
In rooms and halls each look says *decide.*
The smallest gesture hides a vast rhetoric—
conscience an old clipping
you pull out time after time
until it turns to powder.
                         Ahead,
around a corner, you sense a flicker,
buried like ore in a sentence no one speaks,
clamped forever in a piece of chalk.
A spoon ignites memories from the universe
of spoons, the tribe of silverware we
follow from house to house. Dim octaves
quiver in the tines of forks, knives
carry messages along their nicked edges.
Only the familiar surges, slow tides
of frightened wit, words reined-in
before they cut. Each man then,
surrounded by enemies, dulls his tongue,
brings his mind to curl around

the commonplace passed back and forth
like salt and pepper.
                    I travel:
some flake of memory makes me fly
free of work, pulled out of the day
like a hair. Inside, a voice heard
long ago, singing of high tension wires,
sounds of unseen birds. I float
with lost kites, sadness piercing me,
a needle for each pore . . .
                         Noises
like the voices of people wearing gags
rise from artifacts: desk and chair,
doorknob, file—the small helpless
cries of the kidnapped. Furniture
kneels like trussed animals, flowers
wear leaves like the skin of
the dead.
           Even our music is only
the sound of magazine pages turning,
coughs caught in the hand, matches
struck with a pickpocket's caution.
I am here and not here.
A flicker comes to rest in the window
on an apple. I see whole families living there.
Generations pass in afternoon stillness.

Scattered clues follow me home,
the closing door resonant as a cello,
the whining hinge a song
for all the doors I've walked through.
The room is thick: chairs hold presences
and the wind speaks of others
breathing frost on the windows,
trying to draw pictures of the dead.
And next door the house moans
sick as an old soldier

dreaming of a childhood lost
in the hills. My house crouches,
curled like a hand around a match,
my lamp, my ghost on the snow.
No contentment rests in the dim
pleasures of fishbowls next door,
in all the subtly darkened rooms,
in those diligent and talented
sleepers. The house moans
around them, its eyes stitched shut
as their eyes roll and roll
and dreams speed by like trains.
I ride the single island of light
on the street. Beyond it
objects lose color and outline,
fade to fine powders
to feed buried gardens
and the sleeping worms
that ask for nothing.
This is the tropics of the simple.
Each toy pulls its owner away.
All those now tasting sweetness
disappear, flashpowder lives
snapped up like bargains.

Quest

Driven like a fugitive through splintered shadows
I searched all night
for my old houses—
for the other life, the buried one, the lost vanished life.

Where did it live? What was its address?

I worked my way down cold alleys
numbly as an old man threading a needle;
I crossed at the dangerous corners
and passed empty schoolyards
guarded by cyclone fences,
a drone behind slate windows.

Once we dreamed and woke to another dream:
fishflutter of leaves, sun throbbing dust awake,
the warm stone's shape invented by our fingers.

I entered a door and my hand remembered
a loose bolt, my foot nudged a cracked tile alive
and slid familiar as a broom over the worn threshold.
Again I met the mysteries of cupboards, the prim necks
     of faucets,
the frozen mirror thawed for me.

Upstairs I saw a ceiling light with its knotted string like a spider.
I saw the bed and heard the music of its springs again.
Once touched each object shivered.
They pulsed with my old life, these blind witnesses.

Paths

Walking alone on a strange street
I feel an old excitement,
a stirring like those car trips
in childhood that promised
another life, a new school
of echoes, the dull cargo
of the fool thrown overboard
for good: An old car climbs
the grade on Cabbage Hill
coughing steam, tires tender
as balloons. I remember
the knocking motor and all
around me the great silence
of held breath before we
breathed the icy summit's view.
The freight of memory
lumbers with me now down
all that twisting altitude.
My cardboard house folds up.
I am on the path again
that shows you how to lose.
Ozone's lost taste on the air,
no wind, no stir in the leaves
fears become eyes, an eye
for each weeping knothole,
eyes on my skin like kisses.
Once there were rumors
of dead grandfathers—muffled
voices in another room—
and whispers of others lost
in the woods, smothered bones
turned to twigs overnight.
I felt the force of the woods—
ferns winked starvation's eyes

and the cougar of the dark
padded close, huge yet so
delicate no twig broke.
The cat is always there
in the forest thick as sleep
near the path that leads
to cold kitchens. Deeper still
I remember the dirt road that led
to the old farm and how the car
bucked and rattled like a milktruck
over potholes, the farmhouse
rising and falling, pines dancing
the sky jagged. I waited
for the plank bridge. It seemed
only an armload of kindling
thrown over the ditch deep
with brown water, boards warped
and split and thin as lath to
let us drown. But I knew
that if we fell it would be
farther, not just into brown water,
but farther, deeper, darker,
colder than water.

Like the Poets of Ancient China

We are captives now, prisoners of this
sad air, these terrible rugs,
these chairs that caress and hold,
these surfaces chosen like a new
skin. It's sea-level for us from now on.
Here we practice the cottage
industry of the banal; here we
probe the mysteries of the commonplace.
The work is steady, the pay poor.
But we move that way—bloodhounds
of memory, detectives of the ordinary,
explorers in seclusion. And something
always turns up, something to savor
on long winter nights—the ins
and outs of rumor, the intricate creases
of gossip that hint at some vast
answer if we could only find
the key. It keeps us busy chewing
until all the taste is gone
and it takes our minds off our
troubles too: we know the shadows
near us are alive, we know we're
prey. It's calm but we know
the night is armed. And true,
we live in the house of error,
but we live, you see. There are
regions here no map will ever mention;
there are legends, epics on the heads
of pins. Of course teeth grate
in closets and certainly cold hands
reach to us from drawers.
That's only the domestic gothic—
you have it too, a side-issue.
We're after bigger game. It responds
to nothing but our stillness.

In the Middle

Darkness let go of hills
then turned to mist
and snow dust on those
great humped backs
that brood over Indian
graves and secret springs.

You walked the other
way on sentences like
planks, exploring faces,
the life below surfaces.
And behind all that was
what you now have—

the evening. You look
at dandelions, heads
gray fuzz, and pick
them with watchmakers'
hands only to blow
them away, calling it

confetti for some future
small victory. But
it won't work. Somewhere
during the day you
were beaten, duped,
enrolled in madness;

but there are no signs—
only the spirit of a bruise
around you like smoke,
the ache of the flu
just before it happens,
thoughts like gnats,

nothing will settle.
It was speaking
and not speaking.
That and the razor
edges of hours
and cups, all those

calm minutes. Now
the voices of happiness
whisper, telling you
secrets about yourself
you did not know
and cannot believe.

The house is crowded
as a nightmare
and there are places
to go. You go to
those places. You
come back again.

Other Lives

You see them from train windows
in little towns, in those solitary lights
all across Nebraska, in the mysteries
of backyards outside cities—

a single face looking up,
blurred and still as a photograph.
They come to life quickly
in gas stations, overheard in diners,

loom and dwindle, families
from dreams like memories too
far back to hold. Driving by
you go out to all those strange

rooms, all those drawn shades,
those huddled taverns on the highway,
cars nosed-in so close they seem
to touch. And they always snap shut,

fall into the past forever, vast lives
over in an instant. You feed
on this shortness, this mystery
of nearness and regret—such lives

so brief you seem immortal;
and you feed, too, on that old hope—
dim as a half-remembered
phone number—that somewhere

people are as you were always
told they were—people who swim
in certainty, who believe, who age
with precision, growing gray like

actors in a high school play.

Thought darts inward like a tongue
and tastes the pale atmosphere
of the past. But it's like a dream.
The faces have no features.
The rooms are all unfurnished.
We live in daylight now
and travel by standing still,
history coiled in the local, in data
our eyes gather at a window,
not in letters stamped strange
with time and distance
sent from a lost world.
In a stranger's house we feel
the burglar's thrill, the special
pleasure of the trespasser
stepping lightly on forbidden
ground. Only our faces swim
the surfaces of mirrors
and there are no ghosts
for us, no footsteps,
no Other fumbling locks or foraging
the midnight kitchen. Late at night
we prowl at will. We run
our hands over anything we choose.
We read all their books like thieves!

Unlocking the Door

Dead time is heavy
as the dead air,
lost months caught
with the bodies of insects

that darken a light
fixture. All that frenzy
of wings, that buzz,
that beating against

light and heat
now only a frayed
shadow on the way
to dust. I listen though

for wingbeat and whirr
but the air holds
still and the silence
seems yellowed,

damp, so quiet
we speak louder
than usual, turn up
volumes, walk heavily.

There are no messages
here. The last song
died of old age
waiting for us

to come back,
and the air is
thick as some crop
our bodies must

cut. The door's
last slam still echoes
dimly in the highest
corner of the attic—

the spider still quivering,
still afraid. We only know
we must nurse
the deadness from the air

so we may breathe.

There are people inside
as pale as these windows:
wraiths, men and women
of gauze, children

like curtains, floating,
curling in the smallest
draft. Delicate
as insects, they make

no sounds, speaking
with signs, fingers
waving like tiny
banners. Their features

are printed
on their heads; their
genitals drawn on
by children.

Less than paper dolls,
they lead lives
lasting minutes.
Vague cramps

wad them into rags;
heated bulbs
burn them to gray dust.
Their cries as they die

—the only sounds
they ever make—
are like the squeals
of bats or the scratching

of crystal sets.
A few last
two or three days,
making love

by sewing themselves
together and dying
as they rip
out the seams.

Thirst

It comes and goes.
We live with ourselves
for hours every day
and night twists

in our minds—
corkscrew of memory,
our throats dusty
as old playgrounds.

We wait for summer
showers—that smell
of rain-dampened
dust, dryness and wetness

mixed, unheard of
marriages. We have
the dryness, our
partner; we go

fifty-fifty, democratic
for days at a time,
listening to old
stories of ourselves—

back in those great
times when raisins
were grapes. And very
late now the ancient

camels gather on
the lawn, filling
darkness with
laments. They

regret their choice
of occupation,
hate their stupid
humps and want

us—for just
one hour—to
turn them into
fish. We try.

January Thaw

In the mud we
begin to understand.
Fictions fall away—
old skin, old hair,

old midnight pledges
scale in wet light.
Whatever was following
has caught up.

It is with us now.
Old vacancy, old tramp
riding the train
whistles, old ugly

come to visit,
old bastard Daddy
crazy drunk, warbling
hello and hacking

like a bullfrog.
We are his favorites.
His dark pockets
are stuffed with gifts—

Christmas candy matted
with lint and tobacco
is peeled out like ore
and it is just for us.

Rooms

We go from one to another,
crossing sealed frontiers
with ease, our travels eating
geography with great appetite.
This room is Sumatra!
The one behind that door, Nepal!
We walk quickly—
world travelers this evening—
admiring the architecture
of a table, the classic arch
of a doorway, studying native habits,
thumbing through phrase books.
The house swells and our safari
pushes on. The little
throw rugs are islands
and now we are island-hopping.
We run from room to room,
climb Anapurna and bring
our frostbite back downstairs—
a souvenir! We look hard
for some lost thing:
calm, a face, or whatever
alias this thing wears.
We travel to get an edge.
Snapshots are money.
We do all this because
we are the rooms' burdens,
because we are hermit
crabs, because we have
the freedom of the house.
We use this freedom.
We exercise. By god, we travel!

Pioneers

Summer surrounds us tonight.
Leaves are thick on the trees,
the neighborhood quiet, the only
sounds echoes. The streetlight
burns, lynched to its pole
and traffic dwindles to the few
late drunks squinting to keep
curves out of the road.

We are in another house
but darkness is the same old pool
we fish our madness from.
It follows us like a stray
and makes me think of all
the places we've lived, gone now,
torn down, washed loose by floods,
picked up and moved at night

to other sites as if someone were
removing evidence, burning bridges.
The vacancy of those houses clutches
tighter than summer, those rooms
emptied of our signs, stations
on a trail that goes one way.
Our lives are engraved with fingerprints
on old magazines, dented pots,

the dog-eared mystery stories left behind.

Beginning

Lights go off like fires
burning down. Here and there
the ember of a nightlight,
a small flame in a child's room.
The winter moon reveals trees
covered with warts and summer's
jacknife valentines. Leaves gone,
some are twisted, pretending
to be driftwood or hatracks
from skidrow hotels.
This is the background
for sending that invisible
hand over all those vulnerable
places discovered during
the day: the twinge,
a quick pain in the chest,
tender muscles, the slight ache.
'Is this the beginning?'
'Does it start here?' The past gone,
an instant, drained like stream
water full of clarity, light,
ice, the flavor of mountains
that gave you only one thing:
a wetness on your lips, a taste.

Mesh

I resign. The days
turn on their sides
like old cattle—
first one, then
another. *I give my name
away, each letter
a dime-store trinket.*
Great clouds roam
overhead, no shape
at all, only dust.
*Soon my voice will fade,
I'll only whisper
in corners to tricycles
and rubber plants.*
We talk of touching,
do not touch. *Even my
fingerprints will go.*
You stiffen and I
watch you die again
and again whenever I
speak. *From now on
I'll only turn up now
and then as your waiter,
burning my opinions
in flaming desserts.*
You die harder each
time and my voice
grows softer—only
because so many deaths
exhaust me. *Soon
I won't even whisper.*
You die. *I walk away.*
Over and over.

By the Willamette

All day the frantic
mill shouted
wooden tallness
down: Every
tree shall be
a conscript
to the cause
of paper!
But now the slow
rumor of a tug
slides by;
log rafts
huddle in dozing
schools
nibbling shore;
a lone canoe
cuts the surface
like a paperknife
scattering moonlight;
and downstream
the Ferris wheel
in the park slowly
mills the night.

The House at Night

Everyone has gone away, buried
in dreams. It is still. The house
is mine. I let go and fill
the space, moving at first
with the stealth of dust, then
rolling from corner to corner like surf,
inhabiting each square foot,
is packed, pumped up like
furnishing all the rooms. The house
a tire, even the dead air
near the ceiling is mine as I
expand, become a king, a whale,
the royal dragon of possession.
Finally, I am the house, tasting
the wood's swirled grain
in my veins and feeling nails
bite where the blueprint said *yes*.

The Father

He walks late at night among the enamel ghosts of the kitchen—
white blur of the stove, the tall refrigerator like the spirit of
    defensive tackles—
and adds coffee to his cup, feeding wakefulness.
Caffein tightens nerves and he settles in the big chair,
its arms familiar as his own, worn places and stains he has made
like moles seen in the shaving mirror each morning.
The forms of his family move around him in a single shape,
a geometry he can never decipher, some pentagram of the senses.
They sleep. He stays awake, a sentry against invasions by
    darkness.
Registers knock. Vague shapes demand entrance. Stillness quivers
    between each sound.
His ears ready themselves to hear moans and screams down
    the street.

Guarding over the strangers in himself hatched by the late hour,
he senses the push of feelings he thought were lost,
memories sent forward like cryptic communiques
from overrun outposts of the past. The wind jimmies windows.
He listens hard to the seashell sound of quiet.
The house whispers to the trees, its cousins.
Upstairs, his children float, youth bed and cribs like rafts,
and he sees himself below that surface
where faceless creatures swim, their eyes antennae,
their atmosphere thick and heavy as grease.
They say nothing to him. His name is their food.
Tenderness rides out in filaments toward those rafts.
Then the quick weakening of love and fear hits.
Helplessness comes over him like a disease.
The fists he must have dissolve into limp hands, bones like paste.
He knows again how days are measured by injury.

This point, this early hour, is a peninsula he has driven to,
the farthest distance from demands—a delta fear deposits.

Here he must learn to bear his name while remaining the boy
    in snapshots,
thinly disguised in the heavy body he now wears.
And now he understands the men who turn errands into
    getaways,
flying off for good on a loaf of bread.
Like seeing a crack of light in absolute dark
he even understands those who stay and kill each person
    near them.
He understands. The shotgun blast is their only music;
the antidote to their disease is death, divided equally;
the geometry of the family cancelled all at once,
those limbs connected by the thinnest strands severed too,
a shape grown too large to carry in the mind, shattered.
He shudders with the sashes, shaking his head quickly,
    moving thoughts away,
disordering those puzzle pieces to begin again.

Somehow he must find safety from cold, night terrors,
the stilettos of chance, the heaped refuse of lies
at the curb of each day. But protection is most dangerous,
    he knows—
to defend we occupy and destroy.
The tendons in his wrists slacken, cut by need.
The great weight of the world pulls from his grip.
He sees it avalanche down, hurtling in the dark
toward the lives surrounding his, defenseless in sleep.
Or do they sleep? Standing, he goes upstairs to pause beside
    his wife,
to lean over the sleeping children listening to their breath,
riding it like a feather. He bends and touches them,
pushes at blankets, strokes their heads, knowing he must live
by touching, that his name and the names of those he touches are
    never known—
no language stretches that far. They live. They still live.
He undresses in the dark and lies down with his wife
and begins floating through darkness to the shallow glassy
    light of morning.

26

Living

No one tells you how it's done—
you are expected to know—
to, say, be able to get up every day
at an hour when rising is like pulling gauze from a
    wounded eye,
and then laugh, scratch, greedily eat eggs
without ever mentioning those sad lakes, the yolks.
Worse, it's assumed you know who you are right away
and have a name printed on the tip of your tongue, ready.

The fools go on complaining of infinite illnesses,
mapping your mornings with routes of disease,
filling the air with lamentations and the woes of bunions
    or hangnails
and you're expected to take all this equably,
to nod even though the fools go on living, steady as drumbeats,
while the brave are beaten up and the good die like a snap
    of the fingers.
No one mentions this and if you so much as write secretly
on the back of a stamp, "Fools are fools"
you're thrown in jail and told this is your democratic privilege.
It's sacred—like the liquor commission or the Bureau of Love
where you get dog licenses and snakebite serum.
But no one tells you how.

You're expected to fall in step on the street
and reserve your deepest emotions, your tenderest sympathies,
for mannequins without even the suggestion of nipples or
    pubic hair.

And from the beginning words surround you:
glucose, semester, artichoke—they make no sense—
and you're supposed to like the morning paper
with its printed directions for suicide
that tells you the Pessimist Party is plotting mortality.
No one tells you how.

Others expect you to know what to do at all times
and not simply wander around eating plums
or watching fog in the trees.
They expect you to work and, as they say, work honorably
    all morning
and then stop precisely at noon,
forget the vast complicated ritual of work,
eat again, laugh and talk about weather
even if none exists.
And then just as you begin to develop a taste for this indolence
you're sent back to work that might even be dangerous.
And this is expected when some, like you and me,
may find it hard mastering the art of walking up stairs
or spend hours trying to recall our birthstones
or the names of people we're told we love.

And this is only the beginning.
Days come fast.
And you must remember dental appointments
and the size of your hat.
They laugh and prepare cells for example
if you forget and go to work on Sunday;
and there are whispers behind your back
if you call Wednesday a pet name, say, Carburetor.
And if you ask questions so much the worse.
You're lost if you say: Why do you punish your doors
    with locks?

How do you know they like the flavor of your keys?
Or, how many times does a stranger
squeeze your doorknob with a passion
to sit on your chairs so hard they wear out?
Or, does someone want to drink all the water from your taps?

You begin to learn
how it's done
when it's too late;
and at night
if you fall
out of bed
no one cares—
and you even have to teach yourself
the proper technique.

You

You are the secret conscience of the age.
Your power is confirmed
in the milkman's punctuality.
And likewise the paperboy
honors you with paper.
Every day such events
argue the fine print
of your significance
and this says nothing of the seasons—
the way they change—
or the tides or the snow on mountains.
They all pay homage to your majesty.
Indirection is the method—
your name kept secret
for the sake of
Antarctica's integrity
and the sacred ovoid of the egg.
Thus your obscurity legislates.
Everyone reads the volumes of your silence.
Everyone studies your omissions.
Yet you neglect nothing, you take responsibility
for it all; you have high principles
and a strong sense of duty.
Without you the signature of all things
would be illegible. Without you
box-scores would lie
and the seas run dry.
You see this everywhere, these examples
of your strength—the moon
your baseball, the law of gravity
your invention. The mailman's daily passage
says so, the rising sun
affirms it. All bow down, all sing praises
with their actions—

bartender and shoe clerk, the voice
that gives the time on telephones.
All obey.
You are the secret law that all revere,
alpha and omega,
the force that causes runs in stockings,
the absentee landlord of the dust,
the keeper of bees and brothers.
All kowtow.
All sing your praises—
the wetness of rain, the heat of summer,
the blackness of coffee,
the eyes of needles,
the spokes of wheels,
the links of chains.
You see the signs
and are comforted.
The attendant who sells you gas
shows deference.
The grocery clerk speaks softly.
Your breakfast spoon reflects
your face. Your bed
is always ready.
Your omniscience is astounding.
Your key turns and the door opens—
a sign!
Your coins fit slots
in cigarette machines—
a sign!
Signs! Signs! Everything you touch
answers you.
The movie usher calls you "Sir"!

Too predictable — better when walking surrealist edge

Evenings at Home

After dinner you hear footsteps outside
    but they all pass by on their intricate journeys—
  carrying sealed messages to gas companies

but with such deference,
    on tiptoe, speaking quietly
  even to house numbers and wagons.

The same politeness shrouds the house, making you
    smile at furniture
  before sitting down to worry about the carpet—

the way it stretches
    sending pile to every corner—such a flat beached
  fish that only winces when you

step on it, but never whimpers, never even sighs.
    All the objects around you are well-bred, stoic,
  resigned to duties only disaster

will release them from.
    You wait
  for disasters too, some booming

invitation to run in the street, free finally of that
    contract you signed to sit still all the evenings
  of your life.

But some nights you can't stop walking.
    All the chairs point out
  aches, the little bruises thinking brings.

You walk around opening
    and closing doors. Or stare out at
  the faint light on trees

thinking
    of minnows.
  You stop at closets, feel the material of

an old life, look at shoes. And you don't speak.
    Not even
  the need to lie squirms in your

throat. You eat the powder of silence
    and wander toward sheets
  stiff as collars,

the drugged journeys of
    heavy-handed dreams,
  or the bright tumor of sleeplessness.

Riding the Porch

On the porch I smoke
    and watch cars go by—
    few at this hour—
    hitching rides
    in my thoughts
    to any destination.

There is a door somewhere
    that won't ripen
    until my knuckles rap
    and it falls open
    like a blossom.
    But there is no map
    for such a trip—
    only clocks and calendars
    suggest a way: wait,
    listen, grow old.

The night is so still
    no pistol shot
    could waken it.
    I lean back, tagging
    a white convertible,
    wondering where I might
    wake up tomorrow,
    what new life
    I could be planted in
    like a bullet
    buried in a tree.

My thoughts chase
  that white car until
  I stand on a vacant lot
  feeling the tough thrust
  of each grass blade
  and a network of roots
  finer than hair.
  I sense hunger in that field
  dry as lint as I look
  at an old foundation—
  a few boards, nails
  only rust stains—
  and slowly rebuild
  the house and enter
  quietly as an old dog
  with the newspaper.

I live in those rooms.
  Children grow. Old people die.
  Chairs and tables shudder,
  wearing out. I see a place
  near the sink where the floor sags
  and a spot on a window
  someone wore thin with staring
  waiting for me to appear.

The Nursing Home

All furies ended
I live with empty
pockets and nurses'
hands. Every object
around me is soft.
Every hand trembles.
Chalk walls give
no heat. They brought
me back to listen
to watch-tick
and heartbeat.
One is the other.

Once I heard voices,
the sound of children
in a park, swing-creak,
the joy of feet,
and I walked away.
There was a dusty
field and a longing
for sun blast
and white heat
to burn out the haze
knotted in my frown,
tight as a buckle
at the back of my neck.

Beyond trees I
sensed light, some
small fire built
among weeds—
a place for hobos,
old friends, a fire
to ride up my stick
fingers and build
another fire
in my belly's ice.

I walked into summer
like a hunter.
I wanted fire.
I wanted sun-rage
to spill sweetness
through my cold.
The sun was
all I knew.
Then leaves.
All were still.
Paths quivered
with heat and I
moved toward that
warmth, that place
to lie down, that
home of furious food.

What I saw:
children torturing
a snake, a young
mother with the eyes
of a convict,
old men who stumbled
but never fell.
No one I knew.
And I lay down
in tall grass
dreaming of axes
and drunken summers.

Now I slump
in dreams of liquor
bottles filled with pills.
Once I swallowed rivers
to have fish.
Now the afternoon
is dry and I feel
the dusty evening coming
and the night
which cleans nothing.

The Three-Fingered Man

Signs lead me back: scraps of old news, EAT in neon,
a single lost glove, hopscotch squares,
smudges of broken veins
behind women's knees,
the usual criminals in business suits offering E-Z terms,
$AVE $AVE, Rialto and Granada selling dark interiors,
past boneyards of cars, past moss, rust,
burned-over land—each sign
giving darker instructions each day.

This is the place
where tics grow near your eyes,
the land of bunion and heartburn.
Toothaches flourish here
and the wart, the boil, the itch
—afflictions of silence and neglect.

I drive by vacant stores, little neighborhood groceries,
shelves stacked with dust.
No signs in windows any more, no displays,
the meat case cloudy, the deserted counters in shadow,
in shadow the racks where fat loaves drowsed.

Where is the kid who worked after school?
Where is the owner, irritable
with a bloody apron
tight on his belly?
He was so sure of himself, chewing his toothpick.
He knew all about baseball and wrestling.

And here is another abandoned service station—
SEASON'S GREETINGS in the dirty window in July.
I remember the attendant, a man with three fingers.
Now the pumps rust. The intricate tools are lost.
Where is the three-fingered man?

This is daily, daily: houses waiting for wreckers
and pensioners sipping beer in the Yukon Tavern
play shuffleboard all afternoon
trying with all their strength
to keep the puck
from going over the edge
because when it falls
it makes such a hollow sound.

The Journey Begins

Now they are loading the old Ford in the evening, taking too
   much luggage,
too much fried chicken in paper sacks, lost
even before leaving the muddy driveway.
With great care they jammed dirty shirts and underwear in the
   cracked suitcase,
everyone's clothes together, rank and wrinkled, the flanks
of the case already sprung, the lock losing its hold slowly.
Cardboard cartons filled with rusty towels, a half box of cereal,
the iron with the frayed cord go into the back seat
with army blankets and the squat thermos, spout dripping.

The old man sits very still on a kitchen chair while the
   women work.
His wife, near seventy, sighs and trembles
afraid of highway curves—blowouts hover on the road,
some vast clock figures collisions, fiery breakdowns coil
under the old car's hood. All afternoon she
travelled that long highway, conjuring each dangerous inch,
seeing guardrails spring open like gates
and the flimsy car soar and bounce down ravines
so deep no one has seen the bottom.

The old couple know only that their fat daughter has come
to rescue them from his sickness, its confusion, its haze
around them like woodsmoke.
She drove five-hundred miles fueled by her mother's hysteria:
He was dying but still stumbled into town to drink,
swollen hands like mittens around a shot glass.
Drunk, he beat those big hands blue on the woodshed door.
Sober, he said the bar was there to keep him
from sitting like some old woman eating toothless bread and milk
with a baby's spoon hooked around his thumb.

He staggered home by moonlight, screaming through jackpine
for Bud and Ed, both dead twenty years,
to wake up and have a goddamn drink.
So his daughter—forty-five, three hundred pounds—
drove all night, losing count of flats,
splashing water into steam on the radiator.
Even now as they load the car she eats left-overs.
Her hands always seem greasy, the skin around her mouth
    glistens
and her lips shine as if she had just licked them
before having a picture taken.
You were always such a pretty girl, her mother says. So pretty.

The car sags with its burdens, mud high on the fenders like a
    watermark,
one headlight squinting blindly through the gloom.
The suitcase is now loosely tied on the trunk with
    clothesline—
the daughter counting more on balance than tension
in the line to hold it there. It is her way.
Springs lurch as they get in, the old man settling his brittleness
among blankets and boxes in the back.
Now fear of the road becomes worry over the house:
for the old woman every shingle becomes tinder,
every rafter flammable as balsa wood.

They set out in the dark along a dirt road, a blizzard of dust
around them from a passing logging truck.
Soon the old man sleeps.
His daughter counts his breaths in the rearview mirror.
The old woman winces at every branch that looms swiftly
like an enormous hawk above the car,
scrapes and thumps a claw once and is gone.
The car creeps and whines until they reach the cool blacktop,
suddenly free as skaters on the interstate.
But the wrong turn has waited patiently all day
and they take it gracefully, relaxing on the level road.
The old woman even hums and forgets fire.

They drive on, their lone map lost in a sack of fried chicken,
grease spots forming on it slowly, darkening the land.
Chainsmoking and swearing the daughter keeps steering north,
trying somehow to lean her bulk toward the West,
but the road refuses and they go on and on
as the dark smothers the car
and the blazing white hospital sheets recede with each
wheezing mile the old man breathes away.

Sickness in Childhood

He wanders along old streets
and sees himself at eight
crouching in a cellar, dreaming
himself into the blue body
of a fly trapped by the spider.
Outside, clouds flake down.
Trees and grass breathe soot,
houses sheathed with grit.
Discarded cars, hoods thrown
open revealing wires like weeds
sink in the yards. Posters
for circuses that never came peel
from fences; a tiger loosens,
tears free and flies in the wind,
memory's shapeless kite, silent . . .

It was here he found the prize of sickness
hidden behind the faded couch
slumped against the wall like an old woman
squatting over her treasures of dust.
It was there in the kitchen, the cold hall, the bedroom
with its underwater light all day,
its unmade bed looking strangely injured,
an animal only half-alive.
It was in these rooms he felt the tick and catch,
the feathery tickle of fins in his lungs,
the long fingers of bone
that held his breath until the room
crumbled to sleep.
It was on this street.
It was in these rooms his body learned its drowsiness
and the languor of beds
and long days of radio, the dial's glow like oxygen.
For days he did not see the sun,
only its pale evidence on the wall next door.

It came slowly, feeding his pulse a tremor,
the desire to lie still, the need to be alone,
the terror of loneliness.
He felt no need to hide, no need to get home free—
only the lazy wish to be caught.
It came slowly
out of the night's enforced darkness,
out of the poisons of caution his muscles carried.
And slowly his body poured itself away.

There was the far off noise of war
and his love of blood,
the excitement of Extras shouted
in the distance, voices growing louder with disaster,
panic like a shudder through the pavement.
It was a flowering—this love of wounds and guns,
bodies, daring, blood, and the lion roar and tree-like
       clouds of bombs.
They were all with him in the dusty room,
there in the field in back, there in the traffic
at the dangerous corner he was forbidden to cross.
He looked for tanks and beautiful camouflaged half-tracks.
He wanted the war near. He wanted to touch its loveliness.

It came slowly—the hidden gift, the Christmas present
the house would not reveal until it was time
no matter how he searched.
He lived long days with war and caution,
the silent schoolroom, the loud playground.
The warm darkness was full of knives
and the teeth of unseen animals.
He loved this horror
yet he was so afraid of his haunted room
his breath caught,
so afraid he breathed lightly as the hunted,
so afraid his body tried to learn
the final art of stillness.

45

He felt the fine mesh of nets
falling like snow
over his lungs
but he had to plunge deeper,
to give himself away to danger.
Inside he could taste
the pastey marrow of sickness
as ether-thick voices
urged him to dive
into cobwebbed night,
to cross again and again
all the dangerous streets laughing,
thumbling his nose at caution.
Some part of him had to volunteer,
had to be a casualty.
He needed a wound deeper than a bullet.

So the long fingers arrived—
the fin-brush across his throat,
the cough,
the honorable tears.
He enlisted hard
and swam toward darkness,
the deepest secrets opening
as drowsiness wrapped him;
a hazy poison, a sweet poison laved him
and he felt the night's creatures
turn soft as stuffed animals.
His war ended slowly as the taste for blood faded—
in his chest the sound of locks turning—
and he heard the encouraging voices,
the voices of fur, voices like radios tuned low,
voices inviting surrender.
It is easy, they said, so easy now.

Drinking Late

The others have gone, the last voice
clipped in two by the nightlock,
the final laugh choked silent
by the storm door's click.
I study my glass for secret meanings.
The night's sad music settles
and I swim among my own
sweet dregs, flying the flag of myself
over another dead party.
The dying fire still conjures
a few images: the dead year, parted
friends, assassins and saboteurs, lovers
unknown and unknowable.
Embarrassment troubles us more
than cruelty—I laugh and wince at once
sorting my own collection of gaffes,
my year's supply. We're kept awake
by our fool's cap and bells
rattling the round hours hollow.

My thoughts dance on hurt feet
and I take another drink
letting it study me all the way down,
letting it make the easy journey
that puts the nerves to bed
singing fear its nonsense lullaby.
It's time for the pale life, the life
without desire, the life of the invisible.
But there is the damned year to go over—
skimmed, not read with care of course.
Twelve months of error recorded
in ink, each slip of the tongue notarized,
the few windfalls already bronzed

and lost in the toybox. Those Mondays
like burned forests, weeks in the stocks
of a chair, days of stumps and rubble.
But there was also that vision, slim
goldfish, animal grace and spirit
linked, wish and gesture the same
flesh, the sea writing our names with water.

From my sea-view window I wave
December down, wave at presumed beacons
and phantom ships, wave the way
a soldier shipping out might wave
in a bad movie. But no one's there,
only the breakers' dull lather.
I doctor the scene with a little
more bourbon. Party over, bottles emptied
and ashtrays filled with the usual
casual skill, now it's time to invent:
A crowd just outside. I throw open
the window. Faces look up anxiously,
cheeks like porcelain with tears
of adoration. But I am the Pope of Silence
and merely wave—blessing enough
for such lack of restraint. Faces crumble
and flutter away like discarded leaflets,
the beach empty as the aftermath
of another demonstration of impotence.

The party is down to the hard core—
me. *Neskowin, Ecola, Hebo*—I roll
local names on my tongue like pebbles.
California rides up the coast passing
out cigars and wooden nickels.
Neahkahnie. Rockpools harbor
hearsay galleons, doubloons of coral
and bottlecaps. Old fevers crawl, singing
poverty and dollars, summers made
to order, gift shops decked out like

junior proms. But whatever happens
the Pacific still yanks the coastline
in place like a bedspread. There is
delight in this, history swallowed
like an oyster. And then it all returns
to the private, the bleak assertions
of middle-age: giving up cigarettes,
rich foods—denial. We attack the senses
with denial to show our passion.

Our hearts whittled to the size of walnuts!
Yet with an athlete's skill we pour our
feeling in the dark and practice sympathy
by candlelight. Guilt is brought out like
old silver to start the abject parade,
abasement done with impeccable taste.
It shows one's humanity, everyone saying,
"Look how open and honest he is."
I see the dead evening this way, how so
many spin out the sticky nets of their
compassion. But the mesh is wide
and they settle for interior design,
the Byzantine ulcer. Night is now
the skin of a balloon against
the windows but I wave to my crowd
anyway. They are happy. Their team has won.
Their shoulders are notched for heroes,
their hands are paddles designed only for applause.
I close the window and open the bottle.

Taste-buds have memories: afternoon's flint,
the vacancy of three o'clock, the absolute
zero of the world—no wind, only the stir
of old papers, old men with stucco skin,
sex a frown and indigestion—all such
beautiful things drove us inside Monday
after Monday, drove us into cool taverns,
clipjoints, clubs, dives, roadhouses where

we danced on little round tables, on sawdust,
on linoleum, on oiled floors in the mountains
where moose heads stared down
indignantly and mounted fish never blinked.
All night we had the bees of talk,
dragonflies, scorpions fished from glasses,
crickets in the brain while our heroes
for the night fell off their barstools
to cheers and great applause.
I sit back, the dark an envelope, the sea
only a rumor, unconfirmed.

Thought slows, wades through sand
looking for nourishment, windfalls of feeling
nudged to places of honor in the mind.
It's that time of the morning, nursed
into being with care. Now, for a time
the world repairs itself, all cracks healed,
all doom swabbed antiseptic, scars
wiped away like smudges. Worry snores
deeply, stupidity is papered-over with
vast diplomas of intelligence, the mind
like a dart, like a swan, like an eagle's
eye. But then from trying too hard
this passes. Sharks of disorder surface
in the blood, the radio plants
hairline fractures in the skull and I
only want exile—like the poets of China
during 'The Years of Darkness.'
Li Po, this is a night of darkness. If I
could find it I would offer the Moon
a drink but it's mostly a dartboard now.

They knew the vertigo of nothingness—
life a racehorse glimpsed through a crack.
We cower behind our addresses, we cling
to the rags of our names. They were seized
with grief—tombs overgrown with weeds, moss
by the gate, mirrors too dusty to reflect.

Their hearts, consulted, knew no answer.
There was a way that was no way.
This is familiar enough. I toast your
dust with oblivion. You turned down
the world's bribes—sometimes—
and found beds of straw sufficient.
(Beds of straw and a little spring wine.)
We call it interior exile, secretly pleased
to travel without passports, to travel without
moving. You had your beds of straw. We settle
for nailbeds of metaphor and racks of guilt—
mixing cultures. But we think them
furniture enough. You would understand.

In city after ruined city merchants sold greed
and poverty, duckweed flourished
in the wells, snakes nested on the sacred
altars. Pain and ruin are not exotic
and we taste them twice in images
like this. Floorboards creak menace—
the old music. We become our own shadows.
We live by proxy. Yes, yes
and some nights I am scarcely here.
Some nights I must think hard to find
myself. Some force thinks me away.
Some vagueness erases me and I'm
carried into mists, into clouds without shape
or voice. All my aching bulk, the face
I've learned to wear, my solid citizen's
disguise—all this turns powder, then
less, then fog outside a stranger's house.
Some nights it is like this. But not tonight.
I know my way around this room.

I walk around, not staggering, never slurring
a single thought and discover the odd
beauty of eggs and the unexplained wilderness
beneath a chair. And wonder of wonders—
there's still some bourbon in the bottle,
true money in the bank. And somewhere
even at this butt-end, even in these dregs,
the grave of winter and war, breakers
saw toward shore and gulls lift their heavy
bodies like Indian clubs, shrieking at first light.
Sir Echo, how about a belt? Li Po, just a little taste?